# Exploring climate chaos

A view of Hurricane Katrina approaching the USA in 2005. More large hurricanes are forecast in the years ahead.

## Dr Brian Knapp

New Orleans suffered severe damage when Hurricane Katrina struck in 2005. You can see here how badly homes were damaged.

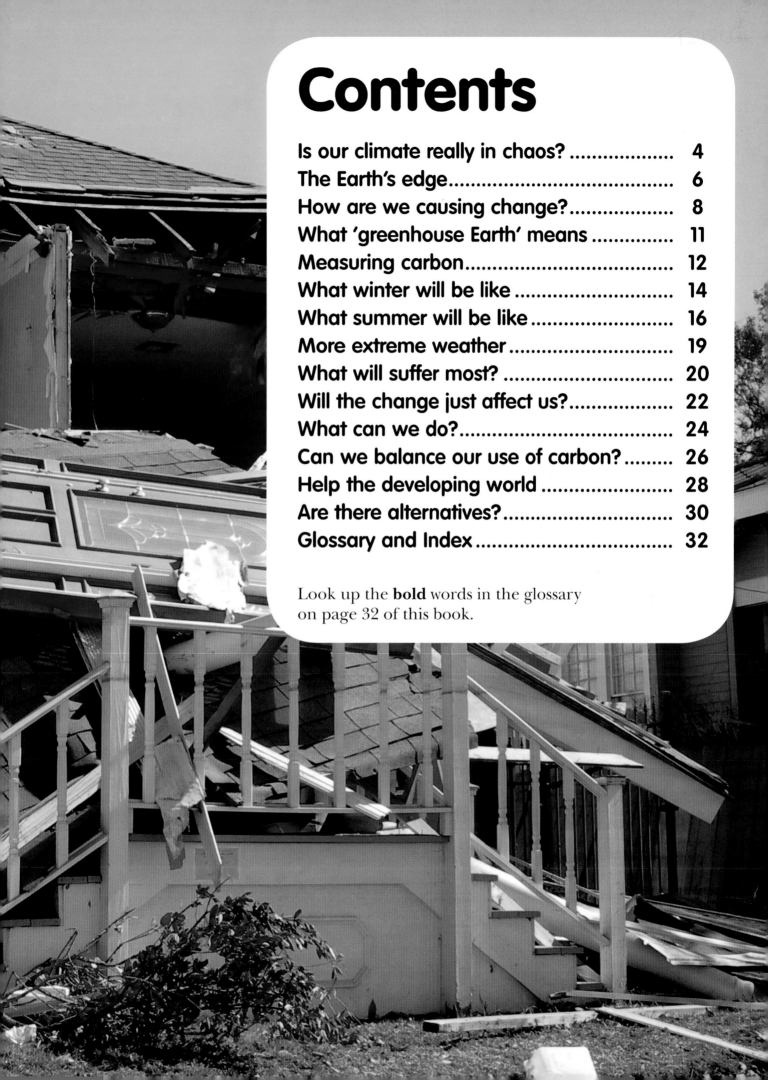

# Contents

Look up the **bold** words in the glossary
on page 32 of this book.

# Is our climate really in chaos?

You may have heard much about the way our **climate** is changing. People don't mean changes from day to day – that is called the weather. What they mean is what we think of as a normal year, will not be the same in the future.

The average kinds of summer and winter we get will change. Some people will face **drought** and be on the verge of starvation.

Others will face far more floods and storms than in the past. This book is about explaining how we have brought about this change, what we can do, and what will happen if we don't.

If the Earth's clouds move in different ways, then some places might get drought and other places might get floods.

## Did you know… ?

- The world's temperature is rising. Two thirds of the rise in the last century has been in the last 30 years.
- The 1990s were the warmest 10-year period since records began in England in the 1660s, and the 2000s are almost sure to be warmer still.
- Sea level is rising by a metre a century.
- Much of the change in climate over the next 30 to 40 years is already set by what we have done in the past. We will just have to put up with it.
- The climate after this will be set by what we do today. So, our future is partly in our hands.

**Q Why are clouds important?**

# The Earth's edge

If you look at the Earth from space, you see a thin, blue hazy band between the Earth's surface and space. This is called the Earth's **atmosphere**. It contains all of the air we use to breathe, and it is what keeps us safe from the direct rays of the Sun. It also helps to hold the heat, saving us from being a frozen planet.

From the ground the atmosphere seems huge. It is everything we can see in the sky. But from space you can see it is very thin. This is why we can change it, and when we change it, we help to change our climate – often for the worse.

This is a view showing Europe.

This is what the atmosphere looks like at sunset if you fly high in the sky. It is the blue haze above the orange clouds. Above that is the blackness of space.

## Did you know... ?

- The part of the atmosphere which has the clouds in is just 18 km thick (just twice the height of Mt Everest).
- The layer above the cloud zone is called the **stratosphere**. It is like an invisible lid, holding our weather and gases close to the surface. It reaches up to 50 km above the Earth.
- The air is made of a mixture of invisible gases. The air is just over three quarters nitrogen and a fifth oxygen. The tiny amount left is mainly water vapour, carbon dioxide and methane. These gases hold the key to climate change.

**Q** What is the atmosphere?

# How are we causing change?

The Earth's climate varies naturally from year to year and century to century, and we have to take this into account. But even so, we have seen a steady rise in temperature on top of this natural change. That is due to us and this is why.

The air is made up of many gases that are invisible, so we can't see them. The oxygen we use to breathe is one of these gases. Most of these gases have no effect on the Earth's heat but some do. They are called carbon dioxide, methane and water vapour (moisture).

Carbon dioxide is a mixture of **carbon** and oxygen. This is the gas that is made in our lungs and we breathe it out. Methane also contains carbon.

These gases soak up heat, making all the air warmer. The more of these gases there are in the air, the warmer it will get.

The gases that contain carbon are so important in this that they are called greenhouse gases.

Burning fires may seem harmless enough, but every piece of coal or log we burn releases carbon dioxide into the air. So when we burn coal and logs, and all other fuels, we should make sure we burn them in the most efficient way, rather than inefficiently, as in an open hearth.

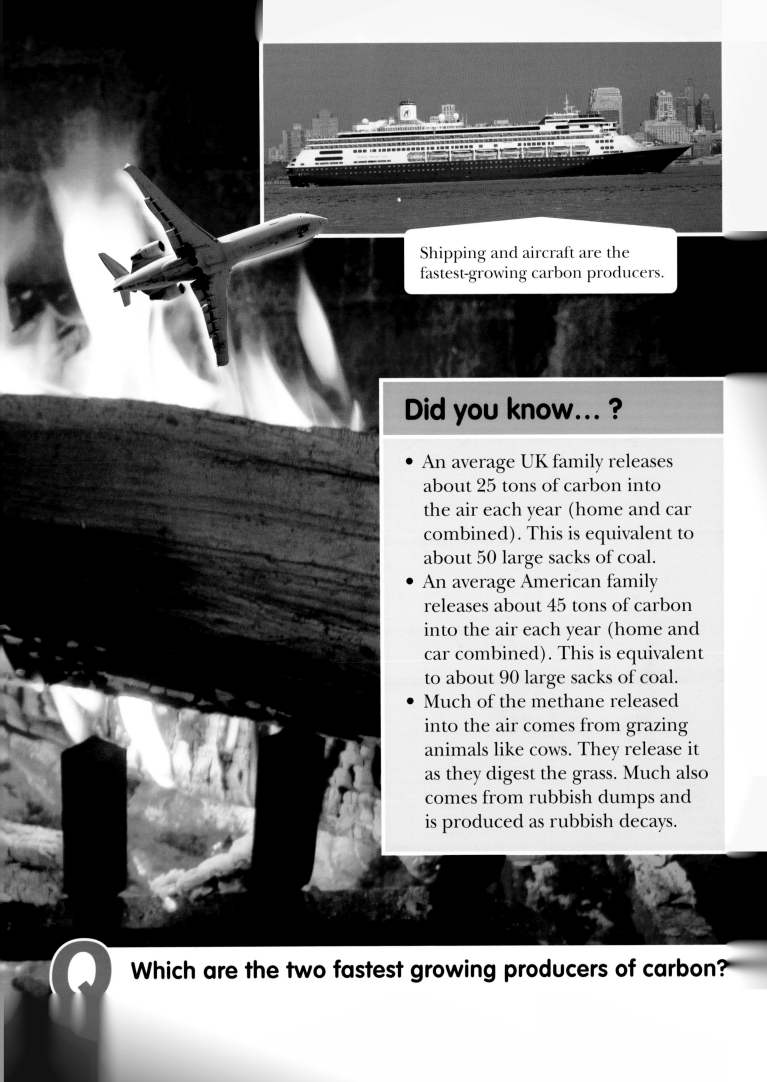

Shipping and aircraft are the fastest-growing carbon producers.

## Did you know… ?

- An average UK family releases about 25 tons of carbon into the air each year (home and car combined). This is equivalent to about 50 large sacks of coal.
- An average American family releases about 45 tons of carbon into the air each year (home and car combined). This is equivalent to about 90 large sacks of coal.
- Much of the methane released into the air comes from grazing animals like cows. They release it as they digest the grass. Much also comes from rubbish dumps and is produced as rubbish decays.

**Which are the two fastest growing producers of carbon?**

Sun

The way that heat moves in the air.

Some heat escapes into space

The Sun's rays warm the Earth

Cloud

# Did you know... ?

- The greenhouse effect is what makes the Earth warm enough for life to grow here. If it weren't for the gases trapping the warmth from the Sun, the Earth would be too cold for life.
- Sunlight passes through the air without heating it.
- The sunlight warms the ground. The heat from the ground is then shared with the air and is soaked up by gases in the air like carbon dioxide.

Earth

# What 'greenhouse Earth' means

In a greenhouse in a garden, sunshine gets through the glass and warms up the air inside. This heat soaked up by the air cannot escape because of the glass, so the inside of a greenhouse gets warmer and warmer. In the Earth, carbon dioxide and methane gases soak up heat, which is why they are called greenhouse gases.

To make sure that the Earth's temperature remains suitable for life, the balance of these gases in the air must not be upset. But we have tipped the balance. When we burn trees, coal, oil or gas, we get energy, but we also put carbon dioxide into the air.

Carbon dioxide is soaked up by plants and trees. The oceans also soak up these gases, but we are now releasing more carbon dioxide by burning fuels than the trees and the oceans can soak up.

 **What is the most important greenhouse gas?**

Some heat that would otherwise leave the Earth and go into space is trapped by greenhouse gases and makes the air warmer.

# Measuring carbon

How do we measure what we are doing? Carbon dioxide is a gas, and coal is a solid, so how do we compare solids and gases? Carbon is found in both of them so we look to see how much carbon is in the air and how much is in coal, oil, natural gas and so on. These measures can be compared.

We then find that the world's people send an incredible 6.5 billion tons of carbon into the air each year.

4.5 billion tons of the total is from burning coal, oil and natural gas for energy. We are also cutting down and burning forests that would have soaked up some of this carbon. This is the same as if we burned another 2 billion tons of carbon each year.

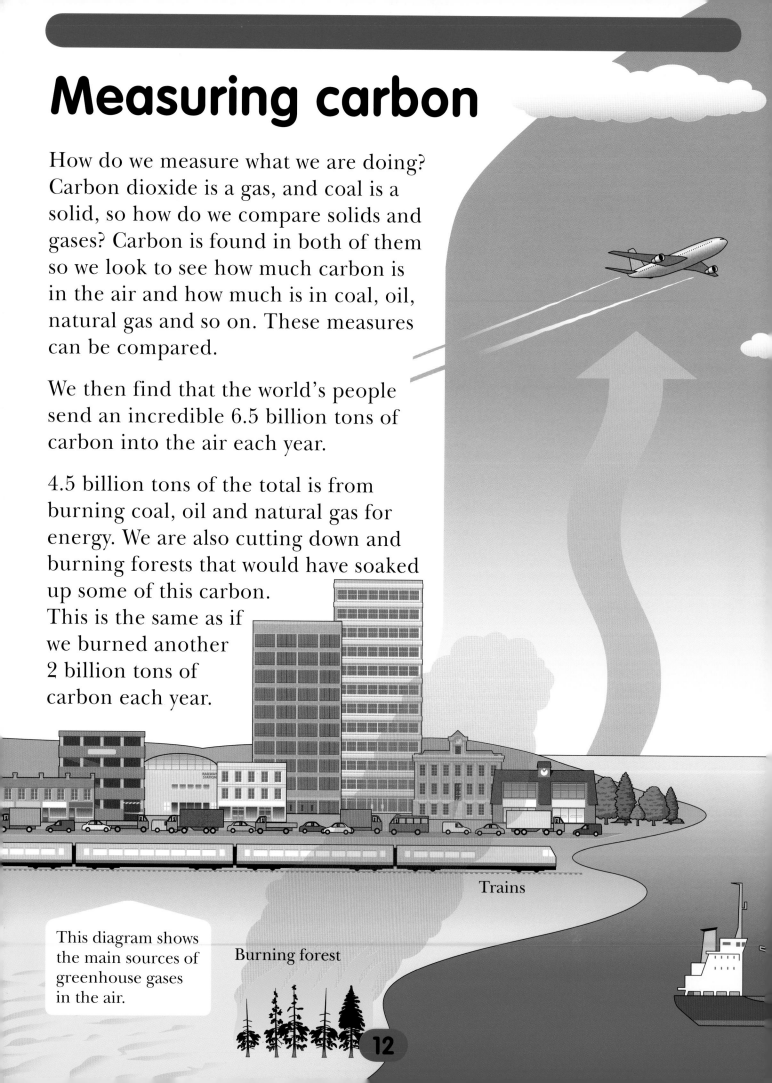

Trains

This diagram shows the main sources of greenhouse gases in the air.

Burning forest

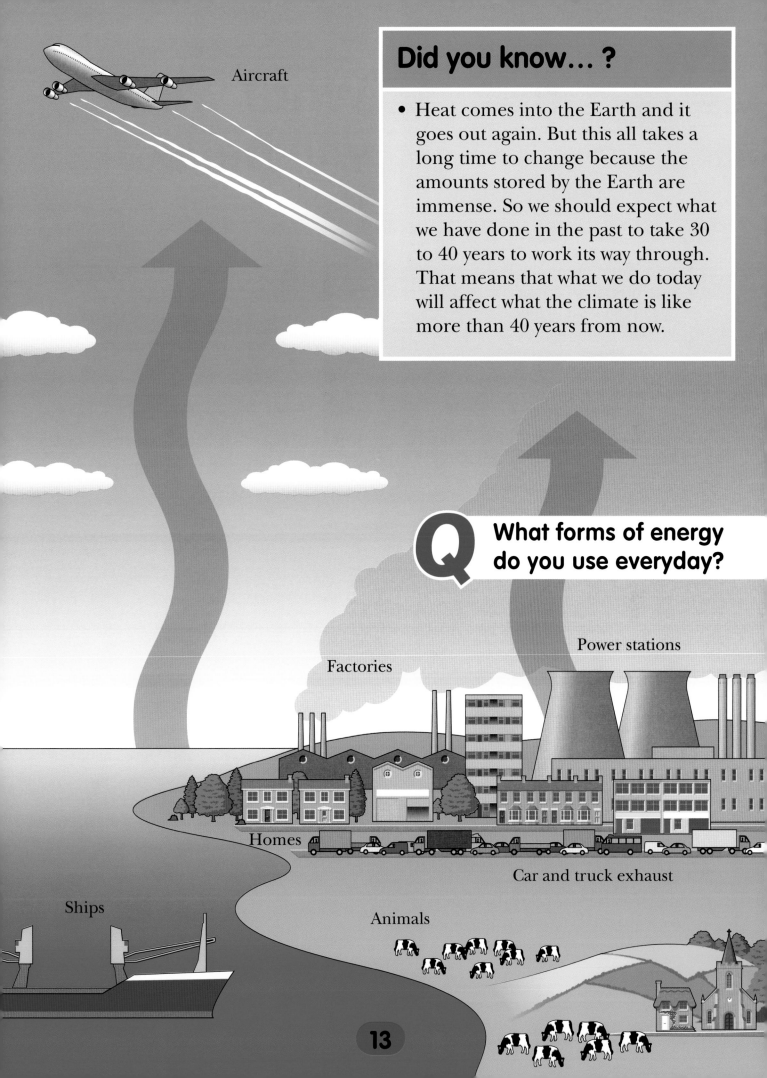

Aircraft

## Did you know... ?

- Heat comes into the Earth and it goes out again. But this all takes a long time to change because the amounts stored by the Earth are immense. So we should expect what we have done in the past to take 30 to 40 years to work its way through. That means that what we do today will affect what the climate is like more than 40 years from now.

**Q** **What forms of energy do you use everyday?**

Power stations

Factories

Homes

Car and truck exhaust

Ships

Animals

With more storms forecast in winter, ships driven aground might well be a more common sight.

# What winter will be like

In the UK winters will be warmer and up to three times wetter.

There will be many more very wet days; the sort of days that make rivers burst their banks and cause flooding.

We will see fewer very cold winters, much less frost, and snowfall will be less. Many of us will not see any snow during winter.

## Did you know... ?

- If temperatures do not fall below 6°C many plants carry on growing and produce their flowers too early. They then get stressed and are less able to grow strongly.
- Lack of snow may be very bad news for the tourist industry.
- More storms will mean that insurance companies will charge more.

In holiday playgrounds like the Alps, the lower ski slopes (pistes) may well not have enough snow for skiing. Snow in the Highlands of Scotland may become very rare.

Autumn and winter will get windier, with more damaging storms.

Winters will get shorter and may not go below the temperature at which plants stop growing (6°C). Winters in the future may be more like the Mediterranean countries get today.

Many ski resorts may have to look forward to an almost snowless winter by the end of this century.

 **How might tourists be affected by climate change?**

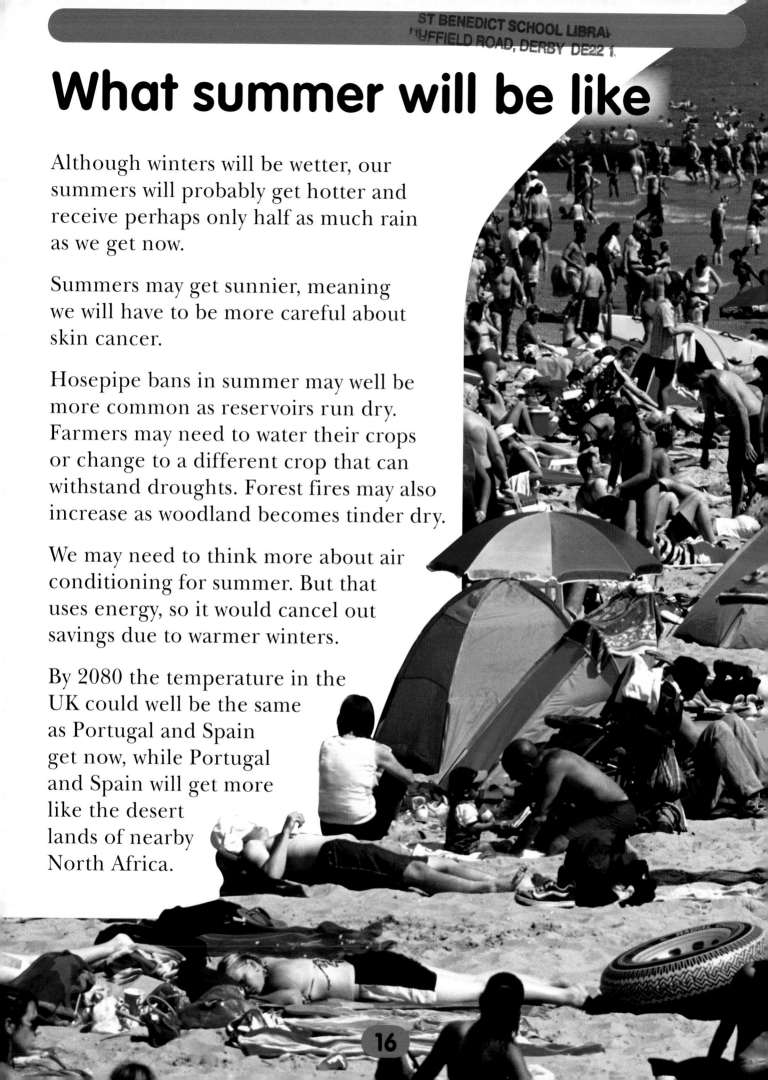

# What summer will be like

Although winters will be wetter, our summers will probably get hotter and receive perhaps only half as much rain as we get now.

Summers may get sunnier, meaning we will have to be more careful about skin cancer.

Hosepipe bans in summer may well be more common as reservoirs run dry. Farmers may need to water their crops or change to a different crop that can withstand droughts. Forest fires may also increase as woodland becomes tinder dry.

We may need to think more about air conditioning for summer. But that uses energy, so it would cancel out savings due to warmer winters.

By 2080 the temperature in the UK could well be the same as Portugal and Spain get now, while Portugal and Spain will get more like the desert lands of nearby North Africa.

Sunbathing at Bournemouth during the 2003 heat wave. Temperatures in the low 30s will probably no longer be thought of as a heat wave in the future.

## Did you know… ?

- We will continue to break all records for high temperatures.
- The warming will not be even: nights will get warmer faster and we will have many hot, sticky summer nights.
- Heat waves will be more and more common.
- Summer will come sooner and last longer into what we now think of as winter.
- Holidaying abroad may slow down as Mediterranean summers become unbearably hot.

**Q** Why might we stop going to the Mediterranean for our holidays?

The hurricane called Katrina which flooded much of the American city of New Orleans in 2005 and blew down many houses happened in a year when more hurricanes were recorded than ever before.

**Q** What else can we expect besides flooding?

# More extreme weather

Sometimes the weather becomes very violent and frightening indeed. Giant tidal waves, hurricanes, tornadoes and floods are all due to the weather.

The reason we will have more storms, more flooding and more hurricanes is that the more heat we put in the air, the more energy there is for the wind to get stronger and for the air to hold more moisture, then get rid of it as violent storms. As the seas get hotter they will get hot enough to start hurricanes more often, too.

Change will not just be in winter winds and storms. It will be in summer heat waves and droughts. Heat waves will become fifteen times more common in the Scottish Highlands than they are today.

More extreme weather doesn't just mean trees blown down. It affects where we shall live. When you build a house you expect it to last for centuries. But in the future we may not be able to build where we have built in the past.

## Did you know… ?

- There is a current of hot water in the tropics that can affect the weather all around the world. It is called El Niño.
- El Niño moves backwards and forwards across the Pacific Ocean every four or five years and can bring unusual floods and droughts. Now it seems to be happening more often.
- The 1997 El Niño had more energy than a million atomic bombs. By the time it had run its course after eight months it had changed weather patterns around the world, killed 2,100 people, and caused at least $20 billion in property damage.

# What will suffer most?

Many wild plants will not be able to stand these changes and they will die, to be replaced by plants more suited to this new weather.

As warmth spreads towards the poles, there will be nowhere for the animals who live in the cold to go. Polar bears, for example, could become extinct.

The world's seas will rise as the warmer conditions make the ice in the Arctic, Antarctica and Greenland melt. The sea may rise by over half a metre in the next 50 years, making coastal cities more liable to flooding. Bigger storms will add to this problem.

## Did you know... ?

- Plants and animals that need cold weather will suffer most and many could die out.
- Polar bears depend on the Arctic sea ice to get out to places where they catch their prey. If the ice melts they will no longer be able to feed, and might starve.

The Arctic sea ice might melt away.

The polar ice cap

**Q** Why might polar bears become extinct?

# Will the change just affect us?

No. It will affect everyone on Earth.

In fact, in our country we will probably get off lightly. It will get hotter and drier in summer, but we should be able to cope.

It is likely that the deserts will grow wider and this means that the billion people living *near* to deserts may, in the future, find themselves *in* the desert as the desert spreads.

Gradually crops will fail and there will not be enough food.

First and foremost, these people will not have enough water. Then they will not have enough food. They will look to us to help them; they will look to move from the lands where they are distressed to lands where the problem is not as bad.

In this way we will all become involved.

Drought means that many plants will die back and there will not be enough food for people or wildlife. As a result, many deaths will occur.

## Did you know...?

- The Sahara Desert is expanding southwards at around 50 kilometres a year. So, if the desert were at Birmingham, it would reach London in three years time. How would we cope? Now you can see the scale of the problem.

# What can we do?

We have already put so much carbon dioxide into the air that things will not get better even if we stay as we are. We have to put less into the air in future. Much less. In fact it means cutting down by two thirds. It is a huge change, and at the moment we are doing virtually nothing at all, so the longer this goes on, the more we will have to change later.

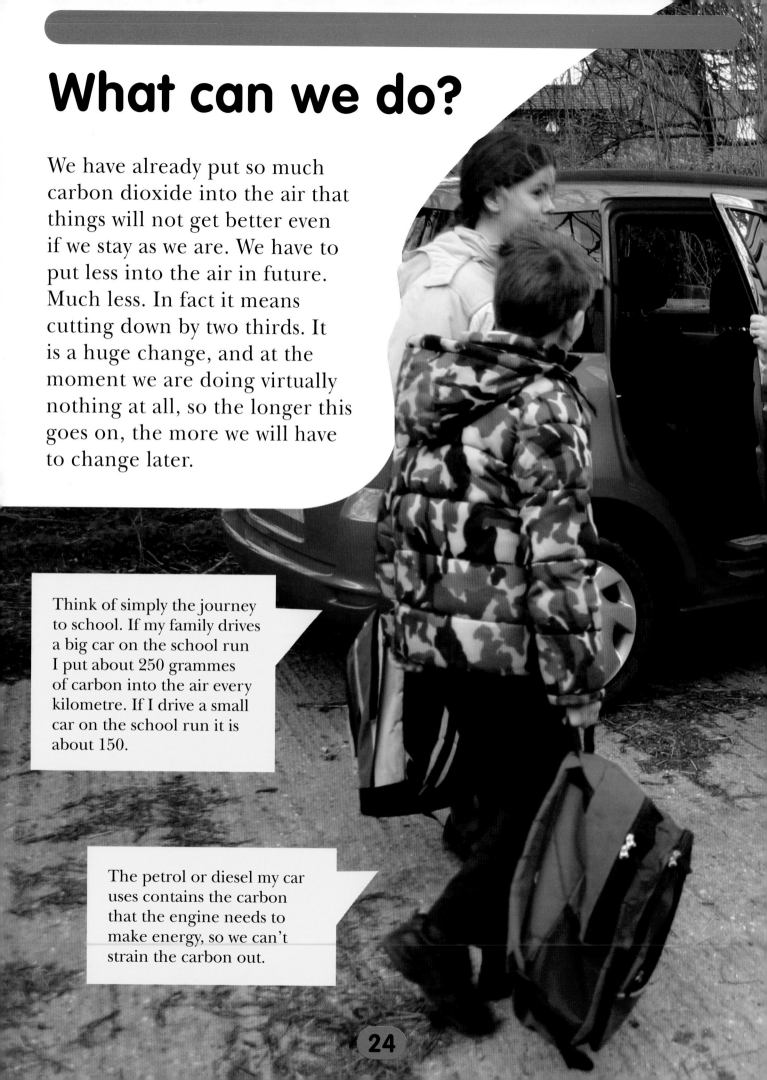

Think of simply the journey to school. If my family drives a big car on the school run I put about 250 grammes of carbon into the air every kilometre. If I drive a small car on the school run it is about 150.

The petrol or diesel my car uses contains the carbon that the engine needs to make energy, so we can't strain the carbon out.

Getting ready for a shared school run.

If I drive 20,000 km a year (an average figure) then the amount of carbon I send out into the air is 20,000 x 250g for a big car and 20,000 x 150g for a small car. That is 5000kg, or 5 tons (5 times the weight of the car). For a small car it is 3 tons, still probably 5 times the weight of the car!

## Did you know... ?

- Idling a car for more than half a minute burns more fuel than it takes to restart the engine.
- Always replacing your car with one that does more miles to the gallon will save carbon, and encourage more economical cars to be made.

So if I drove less by sharing journeys with friends, I would produce less carbon. It is that simple.

**Q** How much carbon a year do you burn on your school run?

It takes time to make giant power stations more efficient because new ways have to be found, so we should NOT look to them to make quick changes.

# Can we balance our use of carbon?

We are putting more carbon into the air than we are taking out. So is there a way to take as much out as we put in?

Some people have suggested that we can balance our carbon. Every company gets a **quota** of how much carbon they can produce. Those companies who send out more carbon can buy 'carbon credits' from those who use less. But it does nothing to encourage anyone to use less.

In any case, it is not just the fault of businesses. Energy companies supply us with oil, natural gas and electricity. So if we demand energy, we are causing more carbon to go into the air. So it is not someone else's problem, it is also ours at home.

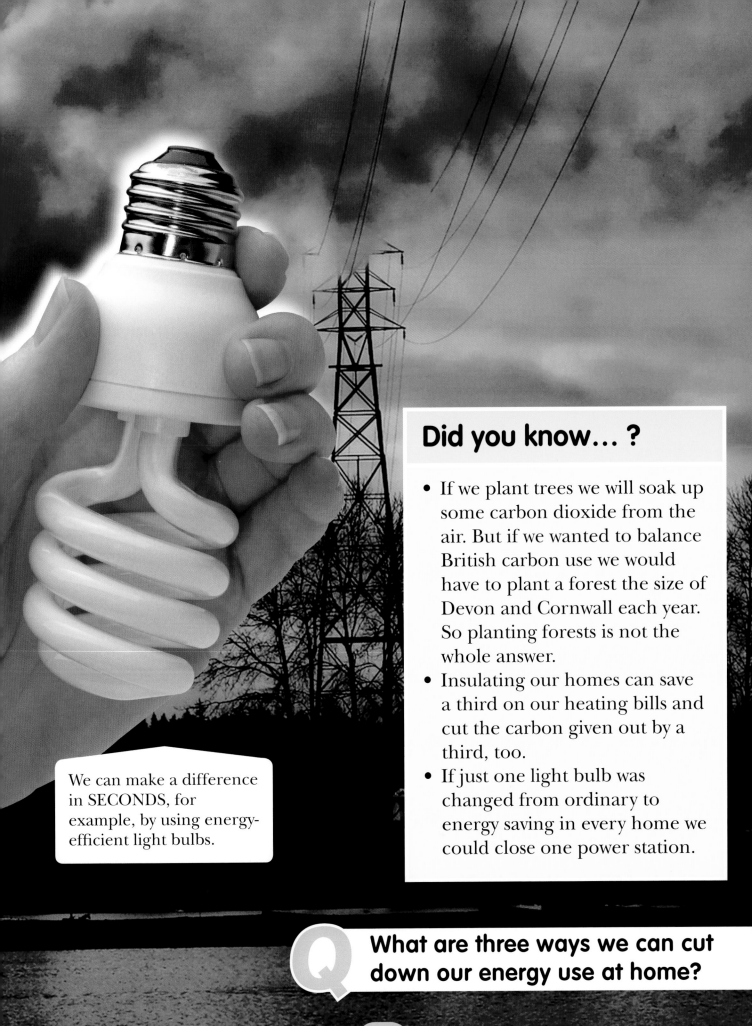

We can make a difference in SECONDS, for example, by using energy-efficient light bulbs.

## Did you know… ?

- If we plant trees we will soak up some carbon dioxide from the air. But if we wanted to balance British carbon use we would have to plant a forest the size of Devon and Cornwall each year. So planting forests is not the whole answer.
- Insulating our homes can save a third on our heating bills and cut the carbon given out by a third, too.
- If just one light bulb was changed from ordinary to energy saving in every home we could close one power station.

**Q** What are three ways we can cut down our energy use at home?

# Help the developing world

We are very fortunate. We live comfortably. We have everything we need.

But other people are not so lucky. However, they now have a chance to get some of the things we take for granted. People in India and China, for example, can now afford electricity when they could not in the past. More of them can afford cars or motorbikes.

Should we tell them they can't have what we have?

Electricity, cars and motorbikes use energy and so give out greenhouse gases.

Soon India and China will produce more carbon than any country (even more than the USA, which is the biggest producer of greenhouse gases today).

As people become wealthier they want cars. As a result, they put more carbon dioxide into the air.

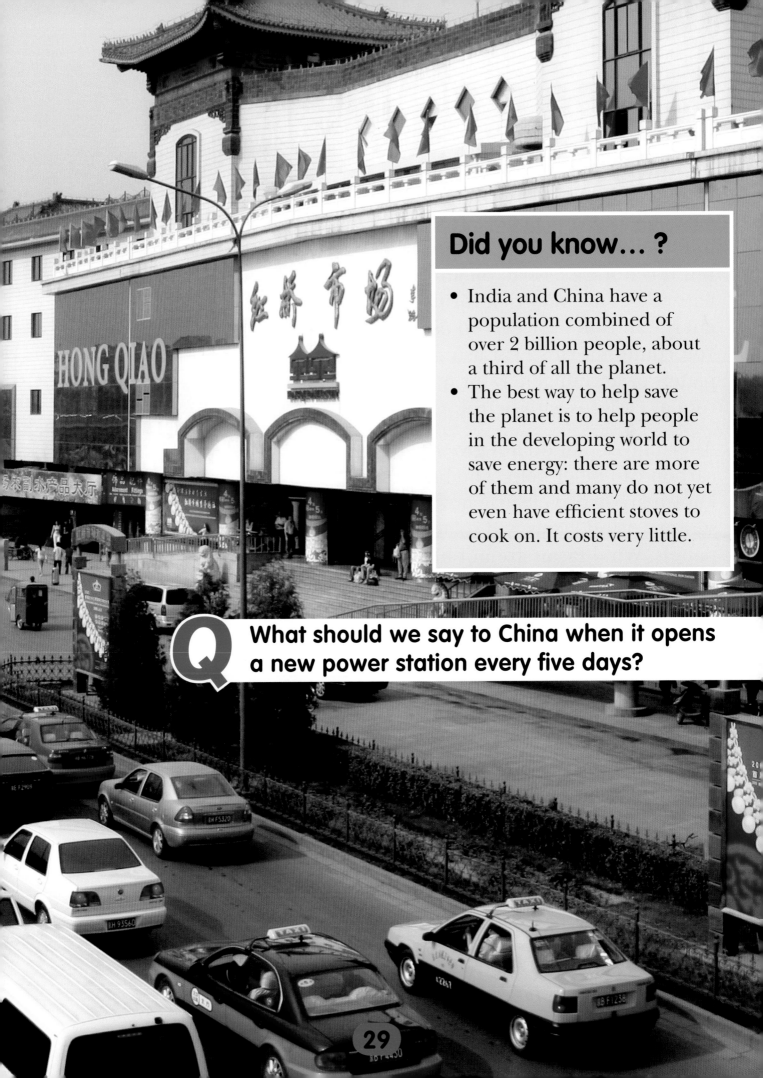

## Did you know… ?

- India and China have a population combined of over 2 billion people, about a third of all the planet.
- The best way to help save the planet is to help people in the developing world to save energy: there are more of them and many do not yet even have efficient stoves to cook on. It costs very little.

**Q** What should we say to China when it opens a new power station every five days?

# Are there alternatives?

Because so much of the problem is caused by burning coal, oil and natural gas, many people are trying to find alternative kinds of energy. But it is not easy. Coal, oil and natural gas are very rich forms of energy and they are easy to use. You could not run a car using solar panels or a wind generator on its roof as easily as with petrol.

Alternatives that do not give out carbon can be of help. The best known are hydro-electric power stations, wind farms and solar panels. Wind farms are not likely to be useful in the long run for most countries. Solar panels will get more efficient as they are developed. Using hydrogen as a fuel may be more promising. Nuclear power is also an option because it does not release any carbon dioxide. We should also remember that if we could make everything two thirds more efficient, we would go a long way to solving our problem.

We can use wind turbines.

We can make more use of the Sun to make electricity.

## Did you know… ?

- If we cut back by two thirds today air temperatures will still rise for several tens of years and sea levels would keep rising for several centuries. It all takes time.
- We could never use renewable energy alone because it only works, for example, when the Sun shines or when the wind blows, yet we need energy all the time. This is why we will still need ordinary power stations and why some people think nuclear power is a good option.

We can harness more rivers to make hydro-electric power.

**Q** Which produces a continuous amount of electricity: wind, nuclear or solar?

# Glossary

**atmosphere** A scientist's word for the air above the Earth's surface. It is made up of many invisible gases. The oxygen we breathe is one of these gases, carbon dioxide that causes climate change is another.

**carbon** Carbon is one of the building blocks of all life. It is called an element. Carbon combines with many other building blocks to make new substances. For example carbon is found in coal and soot. But carbon is not found in black things. It combines to make substances including all of our bodies (bones as well as flesh), all plant tissues, all fuels, carbon dioxide and methane gases.

**climate** The average weather we might expect. Even though the climate is changing, one year will still be different from another. Climate change means that, on average, the years will be warmer, although any one year might still be cool.

**drought** An unusually long period without rain. Many parts of the world have months without rain. This is called a dry season and is normal. But if a time that is supposed to be rainy proves to be dry, then that is unusual and is called a drought. In the UK a drought is often thought of as 30 days without rain. That is because we expect rain every month and so a month without rain is unusual.

**quota** A fixed amount, a kind of ration.

**stratosphere** The part of the atmosphere above where the clouds and weather occur. It acts like an invisible lid, holding greenhouse gases close to the Earth.

# Index

**Curriculum Visions**

Curriculum Visions is a registered trademark of Atlantic Europe Publishing Company Ltd.

Atlantic Europe Publishing

**Curriculum Visions Explorers**
This series provides straightforward introductions to key worlds and ideas.

**You might also be interested in**
Our larger book, 'Weather around the world'. There is a Teacher's Guide to match 'Weather around the world'. Additional notes in PDF format are also available from the publisher to support 'Exploring climate chaos'. All of these products are suitable for KS2.

**Dedicated Web Site**
Watch movies, see many more pictures and read much more in detail about weather-related topics at:
**www.curriculumvisions.com**
*(Professional Zone: subscription required)*

First published in 2007 by Atlantic Europe Publishing Company Ltd
Copyright © 2007 Earthscape

All rights reserved. No part of this publication may be reproduced, stored in a retrieval system, or transmitted in any form or by any means, electronic, mechanical, photocopying, recording or otherwise, without prior permission of the publisher.

**Author**
*Brian Knapp, BSc, PhD*

**Educational Consultant**
*JM Smith (former Deputy Head of Wellfield School, Burnley, Lancashire)*

**Senior Designer**
*Adele Humphries, BA*

**Editor**
*Gillian Gatehouse*

**Photographs**
The Earthscape Picture Library, except (t=top, b=bottom, l=left, r=right): NASA p6–7, 21br, 29; ShutterStock p4–5, 9tl, 14–15, 20–21, 22–23, 26–27, 28–29; US Navy p1, 2–3, 18–19.

**Acknowledgements**
*The publishers would like to thank Heidi, Madeleine and Emilia Allen, and Kezia and Jared Humphries*

**Illustrations**
*David Woodroffe*

**Designed and produced by**
*Earthscape*

**Printed in China by**
*WKT Company Ltd*

**Exploring climate chaos**
**– Curriculum Visions**
A CIP record for this book is available from the British Library

**Paperback ISBN** 978 1 86214 212 1
**Hardback ISBN** 978 1 86214 213 8

*This product is manufactured from sustainable managed forests. For every tree cut down at least one more is planted.*

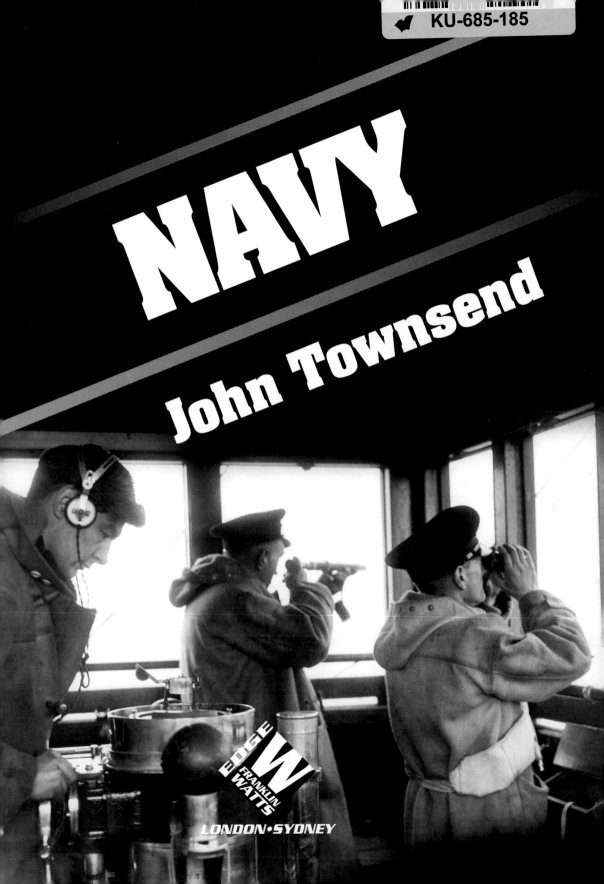

# NAVY

## John Townsend

EDGE W FRANKLIN WATTS

LONDON·SYDNEY

First published in 2013 by
Franklin Watts
338 Euston Road
London NW1 3BH

Franklin Watts Australia
Level 17/207 Kent Street
Sydney NSW 2000

A CIP catalogue record for this book is available from the British Library.

Dewey number:  940.5'41

(HB) ISBN: 978 1 4451 2325 7
(Library eBook) ISBN: 978 1 4451 2570 1

Printed in China

Franklin Watts is a division of Hachette Children's Books,
an Hachette UK company.
www.hachette.co.uk

Series editor: Adrian Cole
Editor in Chief: John C Miles
Art direction: Peter Scoulding
Design: Simon Borrough
Picture research: Diana Morris

Acknowledgements:
Bettmann/Corbis: front cover.
DEA/De Agostini/Getty Images: 5.
GeoEye: 20.
The Granger Collection/Topfoto: 17.
Hulton Archive/Getty Images: 7.
MPI/Getty Images 29.
National Archive/HIP/Topfoto: 4.
Picturepoint/Topham: 9, 27t.
Popperfoto/Getty Images: 11, 13.
2nd Class William G Roy/US Navy: 21.
Topfoto: 1, 6, 8, 10, 27b.
ullsteinbild/Topfoto: 18, 28.
US Naval Historical Center: 16.
US Navy: 12, 19, 23, 24t, 24b, 26.
courtesy of ussubvetsofwwII.org: 22.
Wikipedia: 14, 25.

# Contents

# War at Sea

During the 1930s Adolf Hitler and his Nazi Party became the ruling power in Germany. By 1939 it was clear that Germany planned to take over Europe. When German forces invaded Poland, Britain and France warned Hitler to stop. He refused and war was declared. Other countries soon became involved as World War II spread.

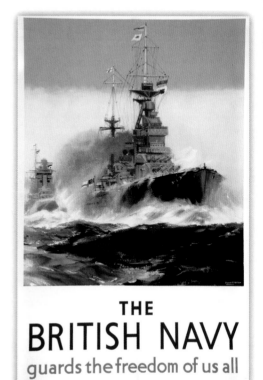

## THE BRITISH NAVY
### guards the freedom of us all

*This Royal Navy recruiting poster shows how important navies were during World War II.*

During the six years of World War II, thousands of ships manned by millions of sailors formed a constantly alert action force on the oceans around the world. The many sea battles they fought had a major impact on the outcome of the war.

Each navy had two main tasks:
- to attack enemy targets (eg ships, ports, shore installations in other countries)
- to defend its own shores from attack, as well as protect sea-lanes and friendly shipping.

Also to ferry troops from place to place.

*Sunk! A direct hit on an Allied warship sends it to the bottom.*

## AF FACTS

World War II lasted from 1939 to 1945 and involved 61 countries.

25 million people in all armed forces were killed; many more were injured.

Allies: forces fighting against Germany and Japan, such as France, Britain and the USA

Axis: the armed forces of Germany, Japan, Italy and others

## ACTION STATS

Size of German, British and French navies in 1939 (full time staff)

| | |
|---|---|
| German navy | 78,000 (approx) |
| Royal Navy | 120,000 (approx) |
| French navy | 160,000 (approx) |

# Hitler's Navy

Hitler was Commander-in-Chief of the *Kriegsmarine* — the German navy from 1935 to 1945. Although its navy was smaller than its enemies, Germany had great plans for building a far superior naval force. This was called 'Plan Z', which aimed to create a fleet of 800 ships manned by 200,000 men.

The Kriegsmarine's most lethal ships were its U-boats ('undersea boats' or submarines). For the first few years of the war, U-boats attacked Allied ships carrying supplies across the North Atlantic Ocean.

U-boats hunted in groups called 'wolf-packs', and fired torpedoes (underwater missiles). These tactics sank thousands of Allied ships during what became known as the Battle of the Atlantic. Allied navies had to find ways of striking back at U-boats.

The ensign (ship's flag) of the Kriegsmarine flying on a German U-boat.

*German U-boats travelled on the surface before submerging to avoid detection and to attack.*

# ACTION STATS

At the beginning of World War II (WWII), the German navy had only 55 U-boats. During the war it built another 1,150. In the Battle of the Atlantic, U-boats sank over 2,600 ships while the Allies sank almost 800 U-boats. Of the 40,000 men who served on U-boats during WWII, 30,000 never returned. This was the highest casualty rate of any armed service in the history of modern warfare.

# AF FACTS

On 3 September 1939, a U-boat fired a torpedo and sank the British liner SS *Athenia* without warning – against the rules of war. Over 100 passengers were killed, but Hitler said the Kriegsmarine was not responsible.

# The Royal Navy

During World War II Britain imported about half its food and all its oil by sea. It needed a strong naval force to protect merchant ships transporting these vital supplies from North America and elsewhere. Much of the Royal Navy's efforts were directed towards protecting the critical North Atlantic sea routes from attack.

*The Royal Navy used fast and agile escort vessels to attack U-boats.*

At the start of World War II, the Royal Navy operated more ships than any other. By the end of the war, the US Navy had become the world's largest.

In 1939 the Royal Navy had 15 battleships, 7 aircraft carriers, 66 cruisers, 184 destroyers, 45 escort and patrol vessels and 60 submarines. Many more of each type were completed during the war.

Not all the Royal Navy's efforts were directed at U-boats. In May and June 1940 it provided critical cover when thousands of British and French troops had to be evacuated from Dunkirk in France.

Canada and the USA helped the Royal Navy by providing escort vessels to protect convoys (groups) of merchant ships from the deadly U-boats. From August 1941, these ships used radar which could detect a U-boat periscope at a range of two km. And in 1942 the U-boat *U-559* was captured with an 'Enigma' coding machine and code books on board. This key information helped the Allies track U-boats and attack them.

*Nazi Germany invaded France in May 1940. A huge fleet of both small civilian ships and Royal Navy vessels evacuated more than 300,000 Allied troops from Dunkirk under constant attack from German aircraft.*

# Case Study: Battle of the River Plate

The Battle of the River Plate was the first major naval battle of World War II. Three of the Royal Navy's ships (HMS *Exeter*, *Ajax* and *Achilles*) took on the mighty German 'pocket battleship' *Admiral Graf Spee,* which was sinking merchant shipping off the coast of South America.

## ACTION STATS

*Admiral Graf Spee*
- Weight: 14,890 tons
- Length: 186 metres
- Max speed: 29.5 knots
- Range: 16,500 km at a speed of 20 knots
- Armament: 6 x 28-cm guns, 8 x 15-cm guns, 6 x 10.5 cm guns, 4 x 3.7-cm guns, 10 x 2-cm guns, 8 x 53-cm torpedo tubes and two Arado Ar196 aircraft

In December 1939, the four ships engaged in a famous battle in the River Plate estuary in South America. The massive guns of the *Graf Spee* scored hits on all three British ships. HMS *Exeter* was badly damaged. The Royal Navy's smaller guns failed to penetrate the *Graf Spee*'s 14-cm-thick steel armour, until finally a shell damaged the ship's fuel system.

*Opposite: the* Graf Spee *on fire and sinking after the battle.*

The *Graf Spee* limped into the neutral port of Montevideo where the captain decided to destroy his ship rather than let the Allies seize it. The captain wrote a letter to Hitler, then killed himself. The end of the *Graf Spee* was celebrated by the Allies as their first real naval victory of the war.

**AF FACTS**

**Germany reported that the *Graf Spee* had sunk an enemy ship and badly damaged two others, while only being lightly damaged herself. In fact, HMS *Exeter* was able to reach the Falkland Islands for repairs.**

*Light cruiser HMS* Ajax, *which took part in the Battle of the River Plate.*

# Battleships

Battleships were the largest and most powerful warships of each navy. They had the thickest armour and huge firepower from large-calibre guns. Battleships were the leading vessels of each naval fleet and rarely operated alone. They were protected by faster, smaller ships.

A group of US battleships, pictured in 1945 at the end of World War II.

When enemy fleets met, the battleships would form a 'line of battle' and manoeuvre to maximise the number of guns that could fire.

After the destruction of the *Graf Spee*, the pride of the German navy was the *Tirpitz* — one of the most modern battleships of the war. With armour over 30 cm thick and massive firepower, this was a battleship the Allied navies had to take seriously. Eventually, in 1944, she was sunk by British aircraft. Huge aerial bombs exploded the battleship's own ammunition and she rolled over and sank, trapping more than 1,000 men inside.

*This photo shows the* Tirpitz *anchored in a fjord in Nazi-occupied Norway. She was found and sunk by Royal Air Force bombers.*

# ACTION STATS

## *Tirpitz*
- **Weight: 42,900 tons**
- **Length: 251 metres**
- **Max speed: 30 knots**
- **Range: 16,400 km at a speed of 19 knots**
- **Armament: 8 x 38-cm guns, 12 x 15-cm guns, 16 x 10.5-cm AA (anti-aircraft) guns, 16 x 3.7-cm AA guns, 8 x 53.3-cm torpedo tubes and four aircraft**
- **Crew: 2,400**

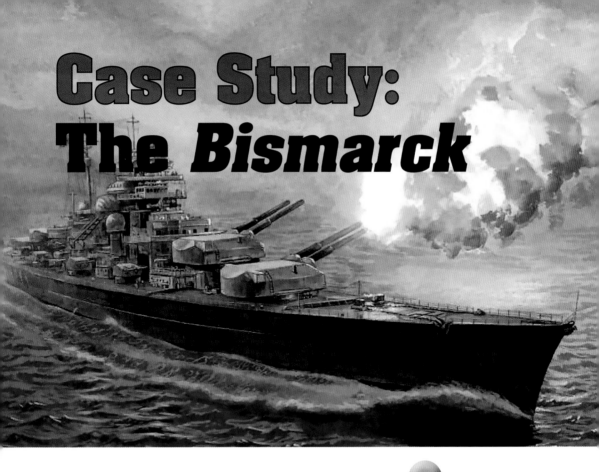

# Case Study: The *Bismarck*

**The sinking of two great warships in 1941 brought an end to the age when battleships were the major forces in naval warfare. Submarines and aircraft carriers took over as the key vessels in the war at sea.**

*This painting shows the* Bismarck *firing its main guns.*

The sister ship of the *Tirpitz* was the *Bismarck* – one of Germany's most famous battleships of World War II. It was a formidable ship. The Royal Navy sent HMS *Hood*, its prize battleship, to attack it in the North Atlantic. *Bismarck* fired its massive guns, smashing a shell through *Hood*'s deck. A huge explosion tore the ship in half and it sank in minutes. All but three of the 1,419 crew were lost.

**Bismarck**
Launched in 1939
Armament:
- 8 x 38-cm guns
- 12 x 15-cm guns
- 16 x 10.5-cm AA guns
- 16 x 3.7-cm AA guns
- Four Ar196 aircraft

**HMS** *Hood*
Launched in 1918
Armament (1941):
- 8 x 15-in guns
- 14 x 4-in AA guns
- 24 x 2-pounder guns
- 20 x .5-in machine guns
- 4 x 21-in torpedo tubes

After this disaster the Royal Navy sent a large force to attack the *Bismarck*. Heavy gunfire from battleships HMS *Rodney* and *King George V* hammered the *Bismarck* until it was ablaze. Finally, HMS *Dorsetshire* fired three torpedoes, and the *Bismarck* sank with the loss of more than 2,000 men.

**AF FACTS**

The Royal Navy was able to sink the *Bismarck* because the German battleship's rudder had been smashed by a torpedo fired by a plane from aircraft carrier HMS *Ark Royal*. The *Bismarck* was a sitting duck.

*Battleship HMS* Hood, *sunk by the* Bismarck *in 1941.*

# Japan Attacks

In the 1930s, Japan built up one of the world's largest navies. This enabled it to invade Malaya and the East Indies for their oil and rubber. However, Japan feared the US might try to stop its plans so it attacked the US Pacific Fleet.

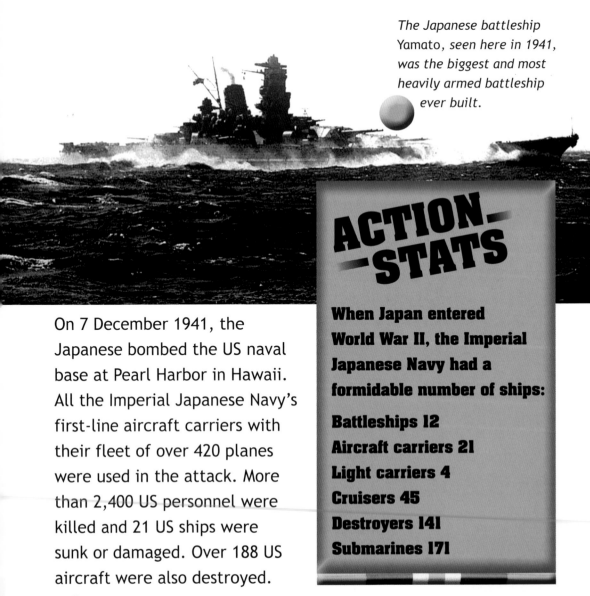

*The Japanese battleship* Yamato, *seen here in 1941, was the biggest and most heavily armed battleship ever built.*

On 7 December 1941, the Japanese bombed the US naval base at Pearl Harbor in Hawaii. All the Imperial Japanese Navy's first-line aircraft carriers with their fleet of over 420 planes were used in the attack. More than 2,400 US personnel were killed and 21 US ships were sunk or damaged. Over 188 US aircraft were also destroyed.

## ACTION STATS

When Japan entered World War II, the Imperial Japanese Navy had a formidable number of ships:

Battleships 12
Aircraft carriers 21
Light carriers 4
Cruisers 45
Destroyers 141
Submarines 171

Until the attack on Pearl Harbor, the US had not joined World War II — other than giving naval support for Allied merchant shipping. Suddenly the USA was forced into the war and within days, other Axis nations declared war on the United States. The Pacific Ocean was set to become a major arena for naval battles with the mighty Imperial Japanese Navy.

Battleship USS West Virginia *burned and sank after being hit with seven aerial torpedoes in the attack on Pearl Harbor.*

17

# The US Navy

After the attack on Pearl Harbor, the US Navy had to recover quickly and engage in the war against Japanese expansion in the Pacific. The first chance they had to do this was in May 1942 at the Battle of the Coral Sea. This was the first naval battle where the enemies fired without their ships coming within sight of one another. Japan, until then seemingly unstoppable, had now been checked.

## ACTION STATS

The US Navy's aircraft carriers operated in the Pacific so that US planes could more easily attack Japanese forces. With 4,500 pilots and 3,400 planes, the US had more airpower than the Japanese navy.

After the USA entered the war, thousands of sailors were needed to man its ships. Posters like this one helped find recuits.

New ships had to be built fast, and the USA had the money and manpower to do just that. By 1945, hundreds of new US ships were in operation, including 18 new aircraft carriers and 8 new battleships — a total of 6,768 ships by the end of the war.

Four huge *Iowa* class battleships were launched to defend the fleet and attack Japanese targets in the Pacific Ocean. USS *Iowa* had fearsome firepower but one of its first missions was to take US President Franklin Roosevelt to an Allied conference in Casablanca, North Africa, in 1943.

USS Iowa *remained a part of the US Navy until 1990. This photo shows the ship firing its huge guns during an exercise in 1984.*

19

# Case Study: Battle of Midway

Six months after the attack on Pearl Harbor, the US Navy defeated Japan in one of the most important naval battles of World War II. The Battle of Midway in June 1942 crushed Japan's naval strength when four of its aircraft carriers were destroyed. The Imperial Japanese Navy never fully recovered from its defeat at Midway.

The US fleet had a naval base on the small Midway Islands in the North Pacific Ocean. The Japanese navy set out to ambush the fleet, then take over the base. US intelligence had already discovered this plan so its ships were prepared and waiting.

The fierce battle that followed destroyed four of the Japanese navy's vital aircraft carriers but only one US aircraft carrier — USS *Yorktown*. Although the US base at Midway was damaged by an air attack, it remained operational and played a vital part in the USA's eventual success in the Pacific.

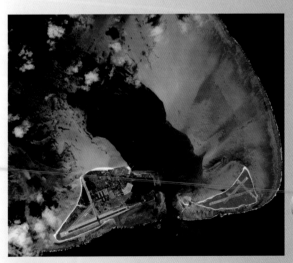

*This aerial photo of the Midway Islands shows the runways of the US base.*

# ACTION STATS

**Casualties and losses:**

**USA**
- 1 aircraft carrier sunk
- 1 destroyer sunk
- 150 aircraft destroyed
- 307 killed

**Japan**
- 4 aircraft carriers sunk
- 1 cruiser sunk
- 248 carrier aircraft destroyed
- 3,057 killed

# AF FACTS

After being hit several times and attempts at saving it had failed, the *Yorktown* finally capsized and sank on 7 June 1942. The wreck was found in 1998.

*Smoke pours from USS Yorktown after being hit in the boilers by Japanese dive bombers at Midway.*

# Subs in the Pacific

World War II submarines were surface ships that could travel underwater for only a short time. Diesel engines gave them a high speed and long range on the surface. However, speed and range were very limited below the surface. This was because the batteries that powered the sub underwater needed regular recharging by surfacing to run the air-breathing diesel engines.

*USS* Balao, *pictured on the surface with some of its crew on deck.*

Japanese midget submarines fill a Tokyo dockyard after the war.

Submarines formed less than two per cent of the US Navy, but sank over 30 per cent of Japan's navy, including eight aircraft carriers. US subs also crippled the Japanese economy by sinking almost five million tons of shipping — over 60 per cent of Japan's merchant ships.

However, there was a high cost — 314 submarines served with the US Navy in the war, most of these being sent to the Pacific. Fifty-two US submarines never returned, nor did 3,505 sailors. This was the highest percentage of men killed in action of any US force in World War II.

## AF FACTS

Midget submarines operated by a crew of one or two were used by navies in WWII. Japan also used suicide midget submarines as well as suicide scuba divers who would swim under boats with explosives on bamboo poles — to destroy both the boat and themselves.

# Aircraft Carriers

The success of aircraft carriers during World War II meant that many navies concentrated their efforts on building this important vessel.

## ACTION STATS

**USS *Franklin***
- **Weight: 27,100 tons**
- **Length: 266 metres**
- **Max speed: 33 knots**
- **Range: 37,000 km at 15 knots**

**Armament:**
- **8 x 5-in guns in twin mountings, 4 x 5-in guns in single mountings, 32 x 40-mm AA guns in quad mountings, 46 x 20-mm guns in single mountings**

**Aircraft:**
- **90–100 aircraft**
- **Crew: 2,600**

*The mighty* Franklin *steaming in the Pacific, its flight deck crowded with aircraft.*

*The wings of most carrier aircraft folded to save space. This is the USS* Essex *pictured in March 1943.*

*Japan's massive carrier* Shinano *remains the largest ship ever sunk by a submarine.*

An aircraft carrier's main function was to act as a seagoing airbase. Each carrier had over one thousand sailors and over 30 aircraft. The US Navy had more than 90 carriers during the war, Japan about 30 and the Royal Navy had 24.

The USS *Franklin*, nicknamed 'Big Ben', was one of 24 *Essex*-class aircraft carriers built during World War II as the backbone of the US Navy's combat fleet. Entering service in 1944, it served in campaigns in the Pacific. The ship was badly damaged by a Japanese air attack in March 1945, with the loss of over 800 of its crew. USS *Franklin* was the most heavily damaged United States carrier to survive the war.

## AF FACTS

Apart from being the largest carrier built at the time, the Imperial Japanese Navy's *Shinano* (above) was the shortest-lived carrier in WWII. On its maiden voyage in November 1944, it was torpedoed by the USS *Archer-Fish*, a *Balao*-class submarine. It kept sailing but lost power and, after eleven hours, the huge ship capsized with all its 1,350 crew.

# Destroyers

When torpedoes were developed in the late 1800s, navies realised they needed small, fast warships to protect their fleets. These 'torpedo-boat destroyers' were smaller than cruisers and, by World War II, had become known simply as 'destroyers'.

## ACTION STATS

The US Navy had 100 new destroyers when it entered the war in 1941. The following year, the first of a new batch of 175 destroyers (the *Fletcher* class) went into action in the Pacific.

USS McGowan *was a Fletcher-class destroyer. It was launched in 1943 and saw extensive service during World War II and afterwards.*

678

This picture shows a torpedo being launched from a ship.

Destroyers became essential for attacking torpedo-firing submarines and preventing them from getting in range to attack cruisers, battleships or aircraft carriers. They also had to prevent enemy destroyers closing in to strike with torpedoes, as well as scouting waters for submarines or mines, often close to shore.

Many ships were badly damaged when hitting enemy mines (floating bombs) in the sea. Some mines were dropped by aircraft. Others were anchored unseen just below the surface. Navies also used destroyers to drag a device that sliced through the mine's mooring line. The mine would float to the surface where it could be shot at and exploded safely. Another method used electrical cables to pass pulses of electricity through the water to blow up the mine.

A direct hit explodes a floating mine, protecting other ships from danger.

27

# Final Naval Battles

Battles in the Pacific Ocean continued to the very end of World War II. As the war in Europe was coming to an end, the USA was preparing for a major sea battle to win the war against Japan. This turned out to be one of the biggest naval conflicts of all, with huge loss of life.

*Deadly threat – a Japanese kamikaze suicide pilot crashes his bomb-laden plane into a US ship during the final stages of the war in the Pacific.*

The battle for the island of Okinawa, to the south of Japan, in April 1945, was a bloodbath. More than 7,000 US personnel were killed on land and 5,000 were lost at sea. More than 32,000 were wounded. The Japanese lost 107,000 men and 7,400 were taken prisoner. Although 16 Japanese ships were sunk compared to 36 US ships, Japan lost 4,000 aircraft as well as its most powerful battleship, the *Yamato*. Nearly all its sailors were killed.

The last Allied ship sunk by enemy action in World War II was a submarine — USS *Bullhead*. This was on 6 August 1945, the day the US attacked the Japanese city of Hiroshima with the first atomic bomb. Eight days later World War II was over.

## AF FACTS

In Europe, Allied troops finally closed in on Berlin in April 1945 and the Nazi Third Reich was defeated. Hitler killed himself and Germany surrendered. VE (Victory in Europe) Day was celebrated on 8 May 1945. Japan finally surrendered three months later on 14 August 1945.

*Japanese officials sign the instrument of surrender aboard USS* Missouri *on 2 September 1945.*

# World War II Timeline

**Some of the key naval events of World War II**

- **1939** 1 September: World War II begins
  September–onwards Battle of the Atlantic
  December Battle of the River Plate

- **1940** 25 May–4 June: Evacuation of forces from Dunkirk
  November Battle of Taranto in the Mediterranean

- **1941** May: Sinking of HMS *Hood* and *Bismarck*
  7 December Japanese attack USA at Pearl Harbor

- **1942** May: Battle of the Coral Sea — Pacific
  June: Battle of Midway — Pacific
  October: *U-559* sunk; Enigma machine and naval
  codebooks captured

- **1943** September: Operation Jaywick — Pacific
  December: Battle of the North Cape — Atlantic Ocean

- **1944** 6 June: D-Day — Invasion of Nazi-occupied France
  by Allied forces
  June: Battle of the Philippine Sea — Pacific
  August: German Battleship *Tirpitz* sunk

- **1945** March-June: Battle of Okinawa — Pacific
  14 August: Japan surrenders; World War II ends

# Glossary

**AA guns** — anti-aircraft guns

**Allies** — countries (US, Britain and its Empire, Soviet Union) opposing the Axis forces

**Axis** — countries (Germany, Italy, Japan) opposing the Allies

**battery** — a set of big guns that are controlled as a unit

**battleship** — the biggest warships of World War II, with the largest and heaviest guns

**calibre** — the diameter of a gun barrel and the shell it fires. German naval guns were described in metric measurements (eg. 38 cm); British and US guns were described in Imperial measurements (eg. 15 in)

**cruiser** — a large fast warship smaller than a battleship but larger than a destroyer

**destroyer** — a fast warship smaller than a cruiser and armed with torpedos; used for anti-submarine and escort duties

**knot** — one nautical mile per hour (1.85 kilometres or 1.15 miles)

**Kriegsmarine** — the navy of Nazi Germany in World War II

**maiden voyage** — very first journey or mission

**merchant ship** — any ship carrying civilian supplies and armed only for self-defence

**mine** — an anti-ship bomb that floats just under the surface and explodes on contact

**neutral** — not joining either side in a conflict

**periscope** — an instrument that allows crew members in a submarine to see above the surface of the water

**personnel** — people employed for a task, such as in the navy

**torpedo** — an underwater missile launched by a submarine or a destroyer

**U-boat** — German submarine – 'undersea boat'

# Index